Grandma, I Love You

by
Patrick Caton &
Deborah Hansen

0 43422 69557 7

Copyright © 1996 Great Quotations, Inc.

Cover Design and Typography by Roy Honegger

Published by Great Quotations Publishing Co.,
Glendale Heights, IL

Library of Congress Catalog Card Number: 96-76131

ISBN 1-56245-262-2

Printed in Hong Kong

For My Grandmothers Millie and Emily:
Thank you for all you have taught me.

And for my mother Arlene:
I have enjoyed watching you be a grandmother
to my daughter.

*Grandparents somehow sprinkle a sense
of stardust over grandchildren.*

–Alex Haley

Mothering is necessary,
but grandmothering is a luxury of life.

—L. Wyse

She openeth her mouth with wisdom;
and her tongue is the law of kindness.

—Proverbs 31:26

Grandmother was sitting in a low rocking chair, with the baby in her arms, bending over it with eyes of worship.

—Laura E. Richards

Surely, two of the most satisfying experiences in life must be those of being a grandchild or a grandparent.

–Donald A. Norberg

*We never know the love of the parent
until we become parents ourselves.*

–Henry Ward Beecher

Never fear spoiling children by making them too happy.
Happiness is the atmosphere in which all
good affections grow.

—Ann Eliza Bray

My Grandma:
Has a lap that is big enough for both me and my sister—
at the same time. But I like it best when it's all mine.

A grandmother is a baby sitter who watches the kids instead of television.

—Erma Bombeck

Who is getting more pleasure from this rocking, the baby or me?

—Nancy Thayer

Our mothers and grandmothers, some of them;
moving to music not yet written.

–Alice Walker

Hug your grandparents and say "I want to thank you for what you've done to make me and my life possible."

–Alex Haley

When grace is joined with wrinkles it is adorable.
There is an unspeakable dawn in happy old age.

—Victor Hugo

It's the little things we do and say
that mean so much as we go our way.
A kindly deed can lift a load
from weary shoulders on the road.

—Willa Hoey

*It is always self-defeating to pretend to the style
of a generation younger than your own;
it simply erases your own experience in history.*

—Renata Adler

The human heart, at whatever age,
opens to the heart that opens in return.

—Maria Edgeworth

My Grandmother took occasion to give me some very good advice with respect to the behavior of hardly grown girls; she remarked that they should be careful not to engross the conversation, and also, that quiet people were always more interesting than loud talkers.

—Ella Rodman

We need time to dream, time to remember, and time to reach the infinite. Time to be.

—Gladys Taber

*Sometimes in the mirror I see
my mother in myself.*

–Jean Anderson

22

Your old eyes so wise, so warm, so real;
how I love the world your eyes reveal.

—Unknown

Grandma was a kind of first-aid station, or Red Cross nurse, who took up where the battle ended, accepting us and our little sobbings sings, gathering the whole of us into her lap, restoring us to health and confidence by hear amazing faith in life and in a mortal's strength to meet it.

—Lillian Smith

What feeling is so nice as a child's hand in yours?
So small, so soft and warm, like a kitten huddling
in the shelter of your clasp.

—Anonymous

25

*A gentle word, like summer rain, may soothe
some heart and banish pain. What joy or sadness
often springs from just the simple little things!*

—Willa Hoey

The case of a first grandchild is more like the conferring of a decoration or order and one is inclined to sit ostentatiously on a twig and preen one's feathers. It's funny, just plain funny, to see your own baby with a baby of her own.

—Mrs. Clipston Sturgis

*Her heart is like her garden, Old-Fashioned,
quaint and sweet with here a wealth of blossoms,
And there a still retreat.*

–Alice E. Allen

Heirlooms we don't have in our family.
But stories we've got.

—Rose Chernin

My Grandma:
Has a drawer in her room that I can look in anytime I want. It has rings and necklaces, little bottles of perfume, scarves and even a slip to put on my hair when I'm pretending to be a bride. Every time I visit I her I get to keep one treasure from the drawer.
But the drawer never gets empty.

Even when frehsly washed and relieved of all obvious confections, children tend to be sticky.

—Fran Lebowitz

Grandparents have a toleration for, and patience with, the boys and girls, that parents lack.

—Margaret E. Sangster

Becoming a grandparent is a second chance. For you have a chance to put to use all the things you learned the first time around and may have made a mistake on. It's all love and no discipline.

—Dr. Joyce Brothers

Nothing is so strong as gentleness,
nothing so gentle as real strength.

—St. Francis de Sales

*From Generation to Generation: If a thing is old, it is
a sign that it was fit to live. Old families, old customs,
old styles survive because they are fit to survive.*

—Eddie Rickenbacker

My grandmothers were strong.
Why am I not as they?

—Margaret Walker

Grandma (Mom)²

Was there ever a grandparent, bushed after a day of minding noisy youngsters, who hasn't felt the Lord knew what He was doing when He gave little children to young people?

–Joe E. Wells

But were you ever young, Grandmother?
I mean, she continued, a little frightened,
"were you ever as little as I am now?"

—Ella Rodman

Grandma's Recipe:
Whatever the ingredients—always add love.

Salute the day with peaceful thoughts,
And peace will fill your heart;
Begin the day with joyful soul,
And joy will be your part.

—Frank B. Whitney

In Grandmother's corner the sunshine stays, golden and bright in the gloomiest days. In Grandmother's sweet benignant face, there's a lightsome look for the loneliest place. And I think the flowers are glad to bloom, in one dear little window of Grandmother's room.

–Margaret E. Sangster

My Grandma:
Bakes the best cookies in the world—and lots of them.
She says, "Oops, one broke. Another reject from
the cookie factory." I say, "Yum!"

I like Grandma because she hugs me good, she's always glad to see me and she makes every day special.

—Francine Haskins

Life has started all over for me, the young years of happiness have come again in a sweeter form than a mother could ever guess. The love and devotion I gave my child I thought I could give no other, but life held a lovely surprise for me—this year I became a grandmother.

—Kay Andrew

The relationship between a grandmother and grand-daughter is a special relationship. It's teaching, telling, giving and bonding. It's learning family histories and traditions, things that have been passed from generation to generation. It's love shared.

—Francine Haskins

Into the woman's keeping is committed the destiny of the generations to come after them.

—Theodore Roosevelt

I suddenly realized that through no act of my own I had become biologically related to a new human being.

–Margaret Mead

My Grandma:
Turns and hides when Grandpa tries to take our picture.
"This many wrinkles would break the camera" she says.
I say, "Grandma, please be in the picture with me.
I want a picture of you and me to keep forever."

We turn older with years, but newer every day.

–Emily Dickinson

Grandmotherhood:
The condition or fact of being a grandmother.

–Henry Bradley
(A New English Dictionary)

*Why do grandparents and grandchildren get along
so well? They have the same enemy—the mother.*

—Claudette Colbert

My Grandma:
Has lots and lots of plants. She has a "green thumb." She lets me help her plant flowers and vegetables in her back yard. My job is to water the flowers and try to stay dry.

The men in this family seemed like garden flowers, sweet and colorful and quick to fade…The women, by contrast, were like weeds—there were so many of them, and they lasted on and on with a minimal flowering, able to subsist on altogether less in the way of space, nourishment and hope.

—Judith Grossman

Her face seemed to open, like a flower,
with each of her grandchild's smiles.

Memories of Grandmother:
Although my grandmother could so easily assume a
stern and commanding air, it was by no means habitual
to her; and the children, though they feared and never
dared to dispute her authority, soon loved her with all the
pure, unselfish love of childhood, which cannot be bought.

–Ella Rodman

Grandmother looked at me, and through the wrinkles of her drawn smile showed me how many ways she loved me.

—Thomas Clary

*More children are spoiled because the
parents won't spank Grandma.*

By the time most of us can really afford to have children, we are having grandchildren.

Life would be infinitely happier if we could only be born at the age of eighty and gradually approach eighteen.

—Mark Twain

*When grandparents enter the door,
discipline flies out the window.*

–Ogden Nash

You often meet the grandparents who bore you about their grandchildren, but never vice versa.

–Evan Esar

Memories of Grandmother:
She loved her housework, and did it with a pretty grace
and quickness; she loved to sit by Grandfather with
her sewing, or read the paper to him.

—Laura E. Richards

Now may the warming love of family surround you
as you go down the path of light and laughter
where the happy memories grow.

Just about the time a woman thinks her work is done,
she becomes a grandmother.

–E.C. McKenzie

In the years since I began following the ways of my grandmothers I have come to value the teachings, stories and daily examples of living which they shared with me. I pity the younger girls of the future who will miss out on meeting some of these fine old women.

—*Beverly Hungry Wolf*

I do not believe in a child world... I believe the child should be taught from the very first that the whole world is his world, that adult and child share one world, that all generations are needed.

—Pearl S. Buck

Grandparents are people who are overindulgent, overanxious and over fifty.

—Evan Esar

Our generation reclaimed the land, our children fought the war and our grandchildren should enjoy the peace.

—Golda Meir

*Truly there is nothing in the world more blessed
or so sweet as the heritage of children.*

—Carolina Oliphant

*For happiness brings happiness,
and loving ways bring love,
And giving is the treasure that contentment is made of.*

–Amanda Bradley

To keep a lamp burning we have to keep putting oil in it.

—Mother Teresa

Love has nothing to do with what you are expecting to get—only what you are expecting to give which is everything.

—Katharine Hepburn

73

So many things we love are you, I can't seem to explain except by little things, but flowers and beautiful handmade things—small stitches. So much of our reading and thinking, so many sweet customs and so much of our well, religion. It is all you. I hadn't realized it before. This is so vague but do you see a little, dear Grandma? I want to thank you.

—Anne Morrow Lindbergh

Your relationships with people begin in the home, where you learn values. It's the responsibility of the family.

—Melbal Moore

*Our children are not going to be just our children—
they are going to be other people's husbands and
wives and the parents of our grandchildren.*

—Mary S. Calderone

*To Angela her grandmother was old but had
not grown older and was never younger.
This is a usual way with grandmothers.*

—Cynthia Propper Seton

The nice thing about grandchildren is that you aren't too busy supporting them to have time to enjoy them.

Grandma's memories will, for me, be in her kitchen, where she was able to love me through all five of my senses.

—Thomas Clary

I loved her home. Everything smelled older, worn but safe: the food aroma had baked itself into the furniture.

—Susan Strasberg

Grandparents are people who come to your house, spoil the children and then go home.

–E.C. McKenzie

*Those who bring sunshine to the lives of others
cannot keep it from themselves.*

—James Barrie

My Grandma:
Reads me books. Her voice is soft and low, and makes
me feel good. She says it's deep, like dark molasses.
I say it's sweet, like honey. She says it's low,
like Grandpa's. I say it's like music.

You can't light a candle to show others the way,
Without feeling the warmth of that bright little ray;
And you can't give a rose all fragrant with dew,
Without some of its sweetness remaining with you.

Mothers:
Grandmothers were made to spoil your children,
it's their privilege and reward.
After all they had to raise you.

Memories of Grandmother:
In grandmother's attic, we ventured to express our
curiosity respecting the contents of various trunks,
parcels and curious-looking boxes. My Grandmother
indulged our curiosity to the utmost.

—Ella Rodman

I cultivate
Being Uppity
It's something
My Gramom taught me.

The closest friends I have made all through life have been people who also grew up close to a loved and loving grandmother or grandfather.

–Margaret Mead

Healthy families are our greatest national resource.

—Delores Curran

To love and be loved is to feel the sun from both sides.

—David Viscott

No cowboy was ever faster on the draw than a grandparent pulling a baby picture out of a wallet.

–E.C. McKenzie

A grandmother is a woman who used to sit up with her children, and now sits up with her children's children.

—Evan Esar

Holy as heaven a mother's tender love, the love of many prayers and many tears which changes not with dim, declining years.

—Caroline Norton

I believe in Grandmothers—
Tall ones, short ones, chubby and thin,
With big patch pockets for hiding things in.
I believe in grandmothers—
Older ones, younger ones, and in-between
Who say we're successful.

When towels are clean!
I believe in grandmothers—
Who give us the moon and show us a star
By letting us know
We outshine them by far!

—June Masters Bacher

My grandmothers are full of memories
Smelling of soap and onions and wet clay
With veins rolling roughly over quick hands
They have many clean words to say.

—Margaret Walker

Grandma and Grandpa were too busy scratching for a living to need books on how to stop worrying.

—E.C. McKenzie

Because grandparents are free to love and guide and befriend the young without having to take daily responsibility for them, they can often reach out past pride and fear of failure and close the space between generations.

—Jimmy Carter

Grandma always made you feel she had been waiting to see just you all day and now the day was complete.

—Marcy DeMaree

*Don't turn a small problem into a big problem—
say yes to your mother.*

—Sally Berger

The family is the nucleus of civilization.

—Ariel & Will Durant

But if a widow has children or grandchildren, these should learn first of all to put their religion into practice by caring for their own family and so repaying their parents and grandparents, for this is pleasing to God.

−1 Timothy 5:4

My Grandma:
Likes to bake "goodies".
She lets me help her mix the batter and
lick the bowl clean when we are finished.

*It is always self defeating to pretend to the style
of a generation younger than your own;
it simply erases your own experience in history.*

—Renata Adler

No one...who has not known that inestimable privilege can possibly realize what good fortune it is to grow up in a home where there are grandparents.

—Suzanne LaFollette

The history of our grandparents is remembered not with rose petals but in the laughter and tears of their children and their children's children. It is into us that the lives of grandparents have gone. It is in us that their history becomes a future.

—Charles & Ann Morse

*By the time a couple can afford to go out evenings,
they have to baby sit with the grandchildren.*

—Evan Esar

*Granny was so important to my life, but for most
children she isn't even around. That's a loss...
I know my own grandchildren tell me things
they could not tell their parents.*

—Chase Going Woodhouse

*Hindered characters
seldom have mothers—
in Irish stories
but they all have grandmothers.*

—Marianne Moore

*If you think spanking is not necessary,
the chances are you're a grandparent.*

–Evan Esar

Grandmothers can be invaluable to the world of little people. In today's world, they are often the only grown-up who has time.

–Dr. James Dobson

*There never was any heart truly great and generous
that was not also tender and compassionate.*

—South

In youth we learn, in age we understand.

–Marie Von Ebner Eschenbach

Joy is a net of souls by which you can catch souls.

—Mother Teresa

With the coming of that little creature,
the world changed once again for Grandmother.

—Laura E. Richards.

Grandmothers have the time they never had as a mother —time to tell stories, time to hear secrets, time for cuddles.

—Dr. M. DeVries

The best and most beautiful things in the world cannot be seen or even touched. They must be felt with the heart.

—Helen Keller

*I got more children than I can rightly take care of,
but I ain't got more than I can love.*

—Ossie Guffy

*When you look at your life, the greatest
happinesses are family happinesses.*

—Marjorie Holmes

Love looks not with the eyes but with the heart.

Family faces are magic mirrors. Looking at people who belong to us, we see the past, present and future.

−Gail Lumet Buckley

In the effort to give good and comforting answers to the young questioners whom we love, we very often arrive at good and comforting answers for ourselves.

–Ruth Goode

Give a little love to a child and you get a great deal back.

—John Ruskin

Grandma's love is a quilt,
warm and secure but never suffocating.

—Thomas Clary

124

If nothing is going well,
call your grandfather or grandmother.

—Italian Proverb

125

To a Granddaughter:
For all she is so tiny,Her strength's beyond compare. She
wraps me 'round her finger and keeps me helpless there!

—Vivian C. Isgrig

Another thing "so simple a child can operate"
is a grandparent.

–E. C. McKenzie

*Once the children were in the house the air
became more vivid and more heated;
every object in the house grew more alive.*

–Mary Gordon

*In Grandmother's day, if she dropped a fork while doing
the dishes it was a sign she was going to have callers.*

I'm a flower, a flower opening and reaching for the sun.
You are the sun, Grandma, you are the sun in my life.

—Kitty Tsui

*Children are a house's enemy. They don't mean to be—
they just can't help it. It's their enthusiasm,
their energy, their naturally destructive tendencies.*

–Delia Ephron

131

I like to think that grandparents have a certain measure of invincibility. They get better with age, never worse. As the toy horse explained to the velveteen rabbit, "Generally by the time you are real most of your hair has been loved off, your eyes drop out and you get loose at the joints and very shabby. But these things don't

*matter at all, because once you are real you can't be ugly,
except to people who don't understand."*
*Grandparents are indeed real. And are they ever ugly?
Surely not, for the children do understand.*

—Lanie Carter

*Some people make the world more special
just by being in it.*

Yes'm, old friends is always best, 'less you can catch a new one that's fit to make an old one out of.

—Sarah Orne Jewett

*...in the home my grandmother created,
I find the beginnings of the love I have inherited.*

—Lois Wyse

Some of our modern grandmothers are so young and spry they help the Boy Scouts across the street.

—E.C. McKenzie

When God allows a burden to be put upon you, He will
put his arms underneath you to help you carry it.

138

From Generation to Generation: Every man is an omnibus in which all of his ancestors are seated.

—Oliver Wendell Holmes

My Grandma:
My favorite part of Grandma is her face.
It has lines all over. When I was little,
I used to call them, "Crinkles."
Grandma says they are wrinkles.
I say they are her story lines.
Grandma has a story for every wrinkle on her face.
Most are about my mother when she was a little girl.

Mother to Daughter:
I long to put the experience of fifty years at once into
your young lives, to give you at once the key which
has cost me tears and struggles and prayers, but you
must work for these inward treasures yourselves.

–Harriet Beecher Stowe

Old love does not rust.
—*Russian Proverb*

*Happiness held is the seed;
happiness shared is the flower.*

Her manner of storytelling evoked tenderness and mystery as she put her face close to mine and fixed me with her big, believing eyes. Thus was the strength that was developing in me directly infused from her.

—Maxim Gorki

*Is nothing in life ever straight and clear,
the way children see it?*

—Rosie Thomas

The real menace in dealing with a five-year-old is that in no time at all you begin to sound like a five-year-old.

–Jean Kerr

Earth's crammed with heaven.

—Elizabeth Barrett Browning

My Grandma:
Has a lap as soft as a pillow. There are no corners,
sharp edges, or bony places that poke me
while I listen to a story.

As I do not live in an age when rustling black skirts billow about me, and I do not carry an ebony stick to strike the floor in sharp rebuke, as this is denied me, I rap out a sentence in my note book and feel better. If a grandmother wants to put her foot down, the only safe place to do it in these days is in a note book.

—Florida Scott-Maxwell

From Generation to Generation:
I love old things: weather-beaten, worn things, cracked,
broken, torn things, the old sun, the old moon,
the earth's face, old ships and old wagons,
old coin and old lace, rare old lace.

—Wilson MacDonald

*As time passes we all get better at blazing
a trail through the thicket of advice.*

—*Margot Bennett*

As long as one keeps searching, the answers come.

–Joan Baez

*In such a time of family mobility and changing family
life-styles, a child needs to learn about his roots,
and the grandparents are the roots.*

—Lanie Carter

Over the river and through the wood—
Now grandmother's cap I spy! Hurrah for the fun!
Is the pudding done? Hurrah for the pumpkin-pie!

—Lydia Maria Child

What you get is a living, what you give is a life.

—Lillian Gish

It is best to learn as we go, not go as we have learned.

—Leslie Jeanne Sahler

*Life is the first gift, love is the second,
and understanding the third.*

—Marge Piercy

*If we could sell our experiences for what they cost,
we'd be millionaires.*

—Abigail Van Buren

Memories of Grandma:
When I sleep at Grandma's house, we make bubbles
in the tub, and we always forget to wash me.
When grandma says, "Tme to get out, your hands
are all wrinkly." I say, " These are my grandma hands,
I like them this way."

Don't you think that the best things are already in view?

–Julia Ward Howe

The family is one of nature's masterpieces.

—George Santayana

...Grandmother's garden was a productive flower garden it was a real storehouse of color and odor, out of which one could, day after day, gather rich treasures, and yet leave its beauty apparently undimmed.

–Samuel Parsons

My Grandma:
She says she's fat.
I say she's round.
She says she's plump.
I say she's comfortable.

Slow. Grandparents at Play.

—Traffic sign from Orange Harbor, Florida
mobile-home park

A married daughter with children puts you in danger of being catalogued as a first edition.

—Warwick Deeping

Nothing is harder on a grandparent than having to watch a grandchild being disciplined.

–E.C. McKenzie